US MILITARY BRANCHES

THE US MARINE CORPS IN ACTION

Percy Leed

Lerner Publications ◆ Minneapolis

Lerner Publications Company
An imprint of Lerner Publishing Group, Inc.
241 First Avenue North
Minneapolis, MN 55401 USA

For reading levels and more information, look up this title at www.lernerbooks.com.

Main body text set in ITC Franklin Gothic Std.
Typeface provided by Adobe Systems.

Editor: Lauren Foley **Designer:** Mary Ross
Lerner team: Sue Marquis

Library of Congress Cataloging-in-Publication Data

Names: Leed, Percy, 1968– author.
Title: The US Marine Corps in action / Percy Leed.
Other titles: United States Marine Corps in action
Description: Minneapolis : Lerner Publications, [2023] | Series: US military branches (Updog books) | Includes bibliographical references and index. | Audience: Ages 8–11 | Audience: Grades 2–3 | Summary: "The US Marine Corps has served the US since it was formed during the Revolutionary War (1775–1783). Learn about marine corps jobs, vehicles, and how they support the navy, army, and air force"— Provided by publisher.
Identifiers: LCCN 2021045402 (print) | LCCN 2021045403 (ebook) | ISBN 9781728458304 (library binding) | ISBN 9781728463612 (paperback) | ISBN 9781728462516 (ebook)
Subjects: LCSH: United States. Marine Corps—Juvenile literature.
Classification: LCC VE23 .L44 2023 (print) | LCC VE23 (ebook) | DDC 359.9/60973—dc23

LC record available at https://lccn.loc.gov/2021045402
LC ebook record available at https://lccn.loc.gov/2021045403

Manufactured in the United States of America
1-50859-50196-2/1/2022

TABLE OF CONTENTS

MEET THE MARINES

A storm crashes into the coast. People need help.

The marine corps brings food, water, and other supplies.

The marines set up and protect bases.

BASE:
a place where people in the military live and work

Then the army and air force use them.

Some marines work on navy ships. They might work on aircraft the ship carries.

Or they may work on ships to be close to certain cities.

The marines formed during the Revolutionary War (1775–1783).

REVOLUTIONARY WAR: when the US fought for independence

They broke up after the war but formed again in 1798.

US Marines in the 1940s

VEHICLE CLOSE-UP

The Cougar 6x6 can go up to 65 miles (105 km) per hour. It can survive small explosions.

UP NEXT!

Working hard.

TRAINING

Marines train for thirteen weeks.

It's the hardest training of the US forces.

After training, marines receive their work assignments.

They usually stay at a base or camp for at least six months.

UP NEXT!

MARINE ONE

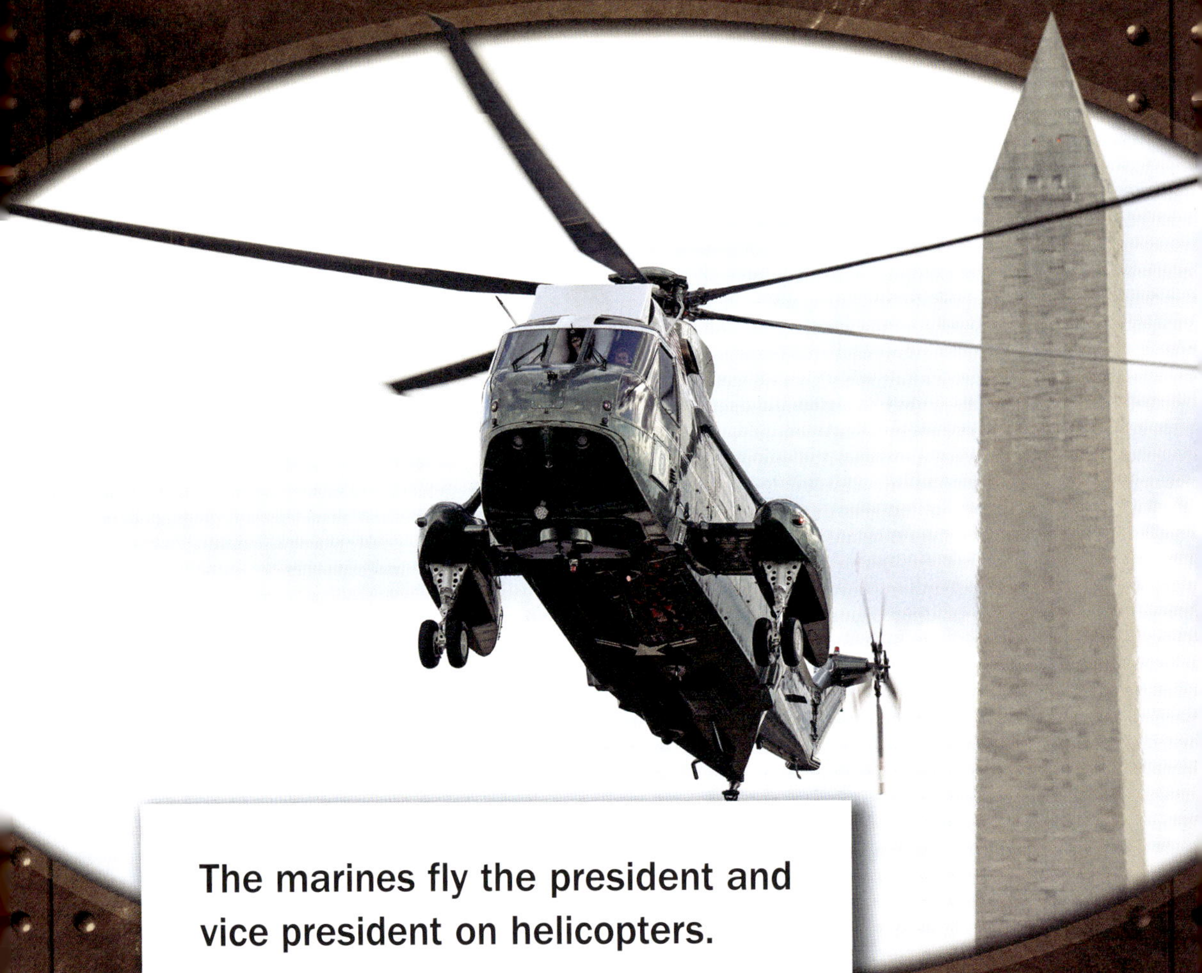

The marines fly the president and vice president on helicopters.

They fly in and outside of the US.

The marine corps is one of the smallest military branches. But they have big jobs.

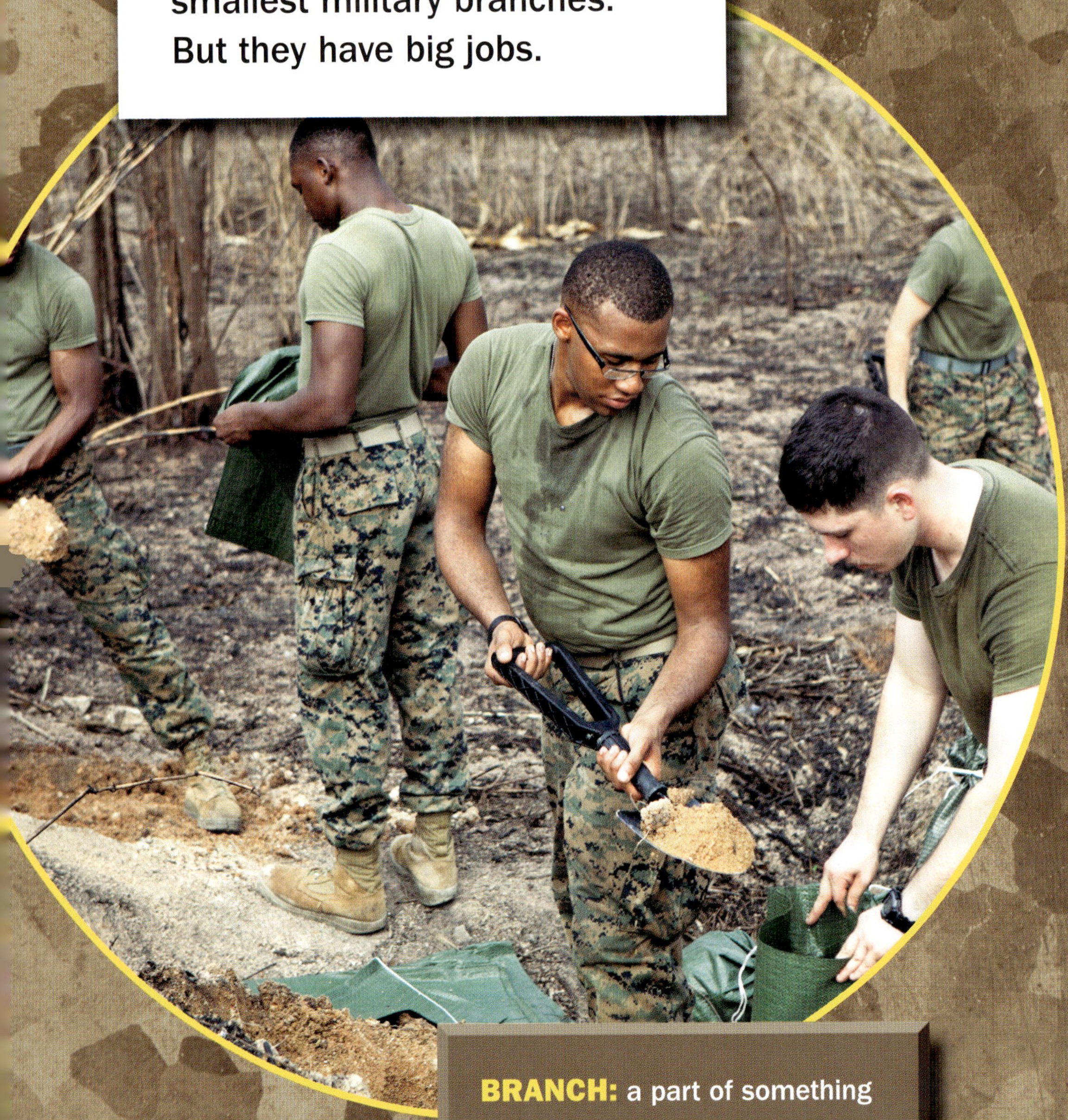

BRANCH: a part of something

MILITARY MISSION

MARINES NEED TO GET SOMEWHERE FAST BY LAND, AND THERE COULD BE SMALL EXPLOSIONS. WHICH VEHICLE SHOULD THEY TAKE?

A. The Cougar 6x6

B. An all-terrain vehicle

C. A navy ship

Answer: A

GLOSSARY

base: a place where people in the military live and work

branch: a part of something

Revolutionary War: when the US fought for independence

CHECK IT OUT!

Ducksters: US Armed Forces
https://www.ducksters.com/history/us_government/united_states_armed_forces.php

Kiddle: Marine Corps
https://kids.kiddle.co/United_States_Marine_Corps

Leed, Percy. *The US Air Force in Action*. Minneapolis: Lerner Publications, 2023.

Leed, Percy. *The US Army in Action*. Minneapolis: Lerner Publications, 2023.

Military Kids Connect
https://militarykidsconnect.health.mil

Rose, Simon. *Marine Corps*. New York: AV2, 2022.

INDEX

PHOTO ACKNOWLEDGMENTS

Image credits: John Linton/EyeEm/Getty Images, p. 4; Lance Cpl. Alexandra Santos Arambulo/US Marine Corps, p. 5; Cpl. Christian M. Garcia/US Marine Corps, p. 6; Lance Cpl. Courtney Robertson/US Marine Corps, p. 7; Lance Cpl. Tyler Harmon/US Marine Corps, p. 8; Petty Officer 2nd Class John Bel/US Marine Corps, p. 9; mikroman6/Getty Images, p. 10; Sgt. Charles Plouffe/US Marine Corps, p. 11; Spc. Derek Mustard/US Army, p. 12–13; Lance Cpl. Krysten Houk/US Marine Corps, p. 14; Sgt. Daisha Ramirez/US Marine Corps, p. 15; Cpl. Savannah Mesimer/US Marine Corps, p. 16; Lance Cpl. Brian Bolin Jr./US Marine Corps, p. 17; Yasin Ozturk/Anadolu Agency/Getty Images, p. 18; Andrew Caballero-Reynolds/AFP/Getty Images, p. 19; Lance Cpl. Adam B. Miller/US Marine Corps, p. 20. Design elements: Andrey_Kuzmin/Shutterstock.com; anyababii/Getty Images.

Cover: Sgt. Branden Bourque/US Marine Corps.